SNEAKY PRESS
©Copyright 2022
Pauline Malkoun

The right of Pauline Malkoun to be identified as author of this work has been asserted by them in accordance with Copyright, Designs and Patents Act 1988.

All Rights Reserved.

No reproduction, copy or transmission of this publication may be made without written permission. No paragraph of this publication may be reproduced, copied or transmitted save with the written permission of the publisher, or in accordance with the provisions of the Copyright Act 1956 (as amended).

Any person who commits any unauthorized act in relation to this publication may be liable to criminal prosecution and civil claims for damages.

A catalogue record for this work is available from the National Library of Australia.

ISBN  9781922641373

Sneaky Press is the imprint of Sneaky Universe.
www.sneakyuniverse.com
First published in 2022

Sneaky Press
Melbourne, Australia.

# Sneaky Jokes

# Volume 3

Sneaky Press

# Why are jokes great?

There are so many reasons that jokes are fabulous including the following:

⇒ Better overall health and wellbeing. Laughter is the best medicine—that's why there are clown doctors who treat sick children in hospitals.

⇒ Jokes provide opportunities to interact with others, building social skills.

⇒ Jokes help build literacy—reading, speaking, expanding vocabulary, identifying sounds, additional meanings and spelling.

⇒ Jokes help build coping skills. They give us an outlet when we are faced with a tough situation—laughing at a joke can help relieve stress.

**What's orange and sounds like a parrot?**

**A carrot!**

# Why did the orange lose the race?

# Because it ran out of juice!

# Why couldn't the skeleton go to the movies?

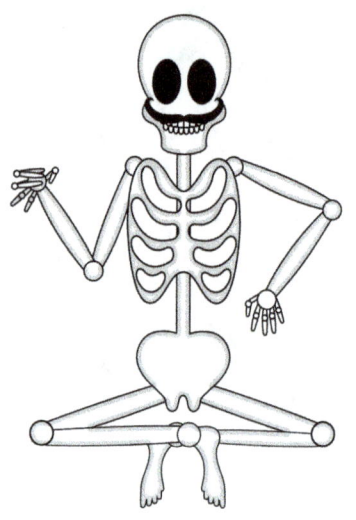

# Because it didn't have the guts!

# Why did Dracula go to jail?

# Because he robbed a blood bank!

# How do you make a hankie dance?

# Put a little boogie in it!

# What do cows read with breakfast?

# A mooooospaper!

Knock, knock.

Who's there?

Boo

Boo who?

Well don't cry it's only me!

# What do you call an ant who fights crime?

# A vigilANTe!

Why did the teddy bear say no to dessert?

Because it was stuffed!

**Why did the student eat their homework?**

**Because the teacher told them it was a piece of cake.**

# Why did the kid cross the playground?

# To get to the other slide!

# What kind of lion doesn't roar?

**A dande-lion!**

How do you stop an astronaut's baby from crying?

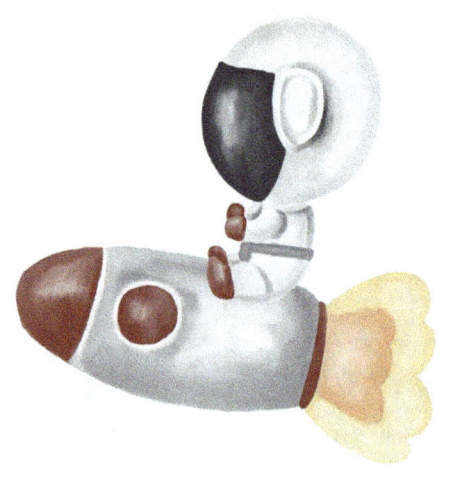

You rock- it!

# What does a cloud wear under a raincoat?

# Thunder-wear!

**Which is faster?**

**Hot or cold**

**Hot. You can easily catch a cold!**

Why was the baby strawberry crying?

Because it's parents were in a jam!

# What is worse than raining cats and dogs?

# Hailing Taxis!

How do you talk to a giant?

Use gigantic words!

# What animal is always at a baseball game?

**A bat!**

What falls in winter but never gets hurt?

Snow!

# What do call a ghost's true love?

## His ghoul-friend!

# What building has the most stories?

# The library!

# How do we know the ocean is friendly?

It waves!

# What do you call a two birds in love?

# Tweethearts!

How are false teeth like stars?

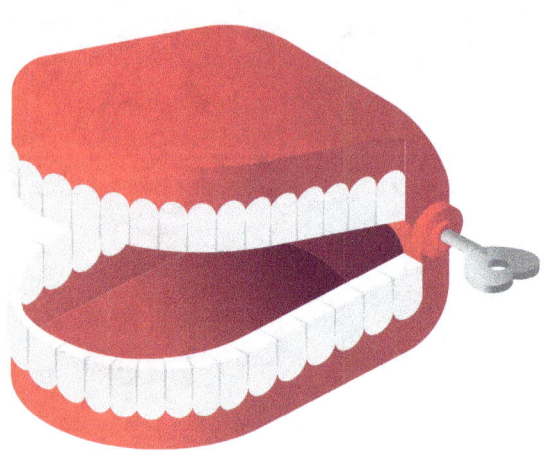

They come out at night!

**What's worse than finding a worm in your apple?**

**Finding half a worm!**

www.ingramcontent.com/pod-product-compliance
Lightning Source LLC
Chambersburg PA
CBHW071550080526
44588CB00011B/1853